Why Judas was Born to Betray
JESUS

Debra L. Griffin

Copyright © 2024 **lilyLuO, LLC**

All rights reserved. No part of this publication may be reproduced, distributed, or transmitted in any form or by any means, including photocopying, recording, or other electronic or mechanical methods, without the prior written permission of the publisher, except in the case of brief quotations embodied in critical reviews and certain other noncommercial uses permitted by copyright law. For permission requests, write to the publisher, addressed "Attention: Book Rights and Permission," at the address below.

Published in the United States of America

ISBN 978-1-963379-48-8 (SC)
ISBN 978-1-963379-49-5 (Ebook)

lilyLuO, LLC
222 West 6th Street
Suite 400, San Pedro, CA, 90731
griffindl@icloud.com.

Ordering Information and Rights Permission:

Quantity sales. Special discounts might be available on quantity purchases by corporations, associations, and others. For details, contact the publisher at the address above.

For Book Rights Adaptation and other Rights Permission. Call us at toll-free 1-888-945-8513 or send us an email at admin@stellarliterary.com.

Contents

Dedication v

Introduction vi

Chapter 1 - **Our Sovereign God** 1

Chapter 2 - **Judas Preordained to His Destiny** 8

Chapter 3 - **Young Judas Iscariot** 14

Chapter 4 - **The Twelve, the Anointed Dozen** 20

Chapter 5 - **Judas and His Deeds** 23

Chapter 6 - **Judas Is in Heaven** 30

Chapter 7 - **The Revelation of Secret Things** 34

Chapter 8 - **Jesus** 39

Chapter 9 - **The Christian Life Is a Successful Life** 50

Chapter 10 - **God's Timing** 52

Chapter 11 - **How Do You Know God?** 55

Acknowledge my baby sister, DIONNE WILSON credit for illustrations

Dedication

This book is dedicated to the body of Christ, the Church within you, Strong and Triumphant. Selah. "Behold, I come quickly" (Revelation 3:11). "I AM the Alpha and the Omega" says the Lord God, "who is, and who was, and who is to come, the Almighty" (Revelation 1:8).

Also, this book is dedicated to my mother, Lillie F. Griffin whose love reminds me that I can do all things through Christ who strengthens me; my sisters Lori (who is believing God for a husband) and Dionne; my brothers Aundra, Walter, Carl, Dorwin, and Jermaine; and all of my other family and friends that I love and value, I hope that we all spend our eternity in heaven *and lastly, to all of my family, friends, brothers and sisters in Christ who have crossed over through death; I hope to rejoice with each of you again in heaven.* In the name of Jesus, I plead the blood of Jesus over you, yours, and all that you care about that is decent and in order. I bind Satan and loose our ministering spirits (angels) to go before us and make the crooked places straight, the rough places smooth, make a river in the desert and a road in the wilderness. When you pass through the water, you will not be alone; God will be there with you. When you wade through the rivers, they will not over take you. When you walk through the fire, you will not be burned nor smell like smoke. Selah.

Introduction

"Thus says God the Lord, who created the heavens and stretched them out, who spread forth the earth and that which comes from it, who gives breath to the people on it, and spirit to those who walk on it" (Isaiah 42:5).

Jesus saves, heals, and delivers. I found this out for myself in 1989. At the age of thirty, while spiritually dead and living a worldly life, I was diagnosed with breast cancer. One day, while I was at work, I felt my left breast after feeling a tingling and discovered a lump the size of a nickel, which lead me to a radiologist for my first mammogram. The mammogram did not reveal a cyst nor anything cancerous. Instead, the doctor labeled it "suspicious," possibly a calcification, and asked me to come back in six months for a follow-up mammogram.

That, to me, was a good report. I would not worry but just go back later. However, that Friday night, while I was trying to relax, I felt strongly impressed to get the lump out of my body. This heavy impression became a burden, and the Holy Spirit and I in a sense talked to each other—not an audible conversation but a conversation nevertheless.

When talking about this encounter to others later, I would say "something told me," And I later learned that this something was the mighty Holy Spirit. The Holy Spirit talks with all of us, sinner and saint alike. Have you ever been driving down the road, taking the same route you always take, and you hear this inner voice that says, "Do not take this way today, go the other way"? You think that does not make any sense, so you do not heed the inner warning and then out of nowhere, a car crashes into you. I believe that this and similar circumstances are examples of the Holy Spirit making revelations to you.

On that following Monday, I did get that lump out and learned that it was, in fact, cancerous. After a lumpectomy and radiation and much fear and torment, I am well. We all know that someday we will die, but we take comfort in not knowing when and how. The breast cancer diagnosis was a fearful and ugly time in my life that could have defined the when and how of death for me.

I first thought I would just die gracefully, but there was nothing graceful about the fear that gripped me. My spirit rose up in me to fight to live, and I had to learn how to do that in Christ.

My desire to draw nearer to God increased, and I asked God into my life and repented for my sins. I said, "Lord, I am willing to be bound by your words, ways, and tradition, not man's ways and not man's traditions." And then I confessed the prayer of salvation.

I remember the intensity of my encounter with the Holy Spirit and from that night forward yearned to know God better, more intimately.

While growing up, I attended church a lot, but I did not know the Lord or the Bible. I did not know what the Word said regarding healing, victorious living, hell, or the indwelling Holy Spirit. I worked and owned a house, car, furniture, and other stuff; yet I did not own a Bible. I was a sinner from hell, not a bad person, but I was lost spiritually. However, grace and mercy were abounding themselves to me.

While I was recuperating from surgery in the hospital, I saw a Gideon Bible in the bedside table, pulled it out, and began to read it. A nurse who worked at the hospital saw me reading that Bible and was impressed by the Holy Spirit to bring her Bible for me to read. Reading this Bible changed my life. This nurse is Gladys Dodd Howard, my friend and sister in Christ, whose Bible I still have and which I used to assist me in writing this book. I admire her steadfast faith in God.

Reading Gladys's Bible was like viewing an instructional video; the level of my understanding and clarity was glorious. I began to consume the Word and learn God's plan and purpose for my life. God became real to me, tangible to me. His love, grace, and mercy were generous and easy to access.

Through my episode of possible physical death, I found spiritual life—Zoe life—which is the God kind of life. *Zoe* is a Greek word for "spiritual life." After mankind fell and was spiritually separated from God through Adam's sin, Christ came in the flesh and laid down his life to give us Zoe life, once again. I was physically healed in my body from breast cancer by God. Physical healing is a part of the Kingdom's benefit. My love for the Father grew, and his love for me began to consume my daily life. I learned to know and hear the voice of the Lord, and I am learning to obey that voice every day.

After watching *The Passion of the Christ*, I was compelled to write this book. I heard the quiet, still voice of God say to me, write a book on why Judas was born to betray Jesus. Having not written a book before nor given much contemplation to Judas, I thought, *How foolish;* but I quickly remembered, "God calls the foolish to confound the wise" (1 Corinthians 1:27).

I also knew that if I gave my efforts to write this book, God would reveal what he wanted to reveal. After all, he is God, and "there is a time and season for everything" (Ecclesiastes 3:1).

This is my prayer for you as you read this book: "Father, in the name of Jesus, I ask you to fill each reader with the mighty Holy Spirit. Shepherd them, abide in them big, and set their life on fire for your good and glory. I pray that their latter days be greater than their former days. Selah."

My Jesus carrying the Body of Christ on his shoulder.

Chapter 1
OUR SOVEREIGN GOD

God has absolute authority and right of dominion over all of his creation. God is the self-existent creator. He has the sovereign right to do whatever pleases him. God's sovereign power has been in existence throughout all time and eternity. He is the sovereign creator and sustainer of this creation. He is in absolute control of all things and all people. The powers of darkness, sin, Satan, and demons and the wickedness of humankind cannot alter the purpose of our sovereign God.

Genesis, chapter 1 tells us that in the beginning, God created the heavens and the earth. The earth did not have any shape, and it was empty. Darkness was over the surface of the ocean, and the ocean covered the earth. The Spirit of God hovered over the waters.

God said, "Let there be light, let there be land. Let the waters under the sky be gathered to one place. Let there be lights in the huge space of the sky, and let the waters be filled with living things. Let the birds fly above the earth across the huge sky." And God saw that his creations were good and blessed them to multiply.

Jesus did not come into being when he was born; he is eternal. He pre-existed. "Do not be afraid. I AM the First and the Last. I AM the Living One; I was dead, and behold I AM alive for ever and ever. And I hold the keys of Death and Hell" (Revelations 1:17–18). God became a human being when the God-Man, Jesus, was born in the flesh by a virgin birth and dwelt among us on earth for thirty-three years.

"In the beginning was the Word, and the Word was with God, and the Word was God. He was in the beginning with God. All things were made through Him, and without Him nothing was made that were made. In Him was life, and the life was the light of men. And the light shines in the darkness, and the darkness did not comprehend it" (John 1:1–5).

Jesus always was God, is God, and always will be God. Jesus took upon himself full humanity and lived as the God-Man on this earth.

He never ceased to be the eternal God and has always existed. Jesus is the creator and sustainer of all things and the source of eternal life. This is so because God the Father, Jesus the Son, and the Holy Spirit are one—the Trinity. God is the self-existing covenant, unbounded and unfettered by all and any earthly limitations. "He who comes to God must believe that He is the Great I AM" (Exodus 3:14). You are reading the truth about Jesus and the foundation of all truth.

Christ's sacrifice for our sins was not an after thought and not something God decided to do when evil seemed as truth. Long before creating the world, the all-knowing, eternal God set the plan of redemption and reconciliation in motion.

Although Jesus manifested in the flesh as a man, he was unique and set apart from all others. Jesus alone possessed and displayed the qualities of the promised Messiah who was to come into the world. Jesus walked among us as a perfect moral character. He is the Messiah who came into the world as the God-Man. His words, deeds, and manner of life and death authenticated his divine mission.

Mary found favor with God to conceive a baby without knowing a man, brought forth a son, and named him Jesus. King David's prophecy foretold of Jesus' greatness, that he would be the Son of the Most High, and the Lord God would give him his throne (Zechariah 6, Psalm 2:7–8).

Jesus would reign over the house of Jacob forever, and of his kingdom, there would be no end. God had given his covenant to David, promising an heir of his would sit on the throne and rule over Jerusalem. This covenant was to be accompanied by a sign that would demonstrate that God had fulfilled his covenant and promise of a Messiah.

"Therefore, the Lord Himself will give you a sign: Behold, the virgin shall conceive and bear a Son and shall call His name Immanuel" (Isaiah 7:14), which means "God with us." For with God, nothing is impossible.

Judas's betrayal of Jesus provided the bridge for Jesus to be crucified on the cross to redeem humanity from the curses of sin, sickness, poverty, and death. Christians are saved by faith and given the opportunity to choose whom they want to serve: Jesus, who gives life and life more abundantly on earth and in Heaven; or Satan, who brings eternal death in hell. Jesus' death and resurrection extols you to choose life, Zoe life.

Zoe is a Greek word for "spiritual life." After mankind fell and was spiritually separated from God through Adam's sin, Christ came in the flesh and laid down his life to give us Zoe life, once again. The plan of salvation is repentance toward God and faith in Christ Jesus. *Salvation* means being born again and going to heaven when we die. It also includes material and temporal deliverance from danger and apprehension, preservation, pardon, restoration, healing, wholeness, and soundness. To be spiritually saved is to say confidently, "It is well," and know that whatever is going on in your world, God will get you through it. Selah.

What is faith? Now faith is the substance, the assurance, the title deed of things seen and unseen and hoped for—the evidence, proof, and conviction of things not seen. By faith we obtain a good testimony. By faith, we understand that the world, heaven, and earth was framed by the words of God, so that the things that are seen were not made of things that are visible (Hebrews 11:1-3). Faith reaches beyond the natural realm of man's ability to possess the supernatural realm. Obtaining and activating faith is the key to successful Christian living. "Without faith it is impossible to please God, for he who comes to God must believe that He is, and that He is a rewarder of those who diligently seek him" (Hebrew 11:6).

To be saved, you only have to "confess with your mouth that Jesus is Lord and believe in your heart that Jesus is the risen Savior" (Roman 10:9-10). Any trust you place in Jesus will never be put to shame. God cannot lie and still be God. When we call upon the name of the Lord God for salvation, we are saved, and all is well.

Repentance is a gift of God's goodness. The goodness of God is not merited by the act of repentance. Repentance, like faith, is a gift. This gift of repentance is an inward change produced by the convicting power of the Holy Spirit as the Word of God washes. Faith in God is strengthened when you hear God's Word; therefore, read and mediate on the Word of God. A sound foundation for a successful Christian life requires that you read and study your Bible and watch what you speak out of your mouth. Do a confession checkup to see if you are speaking words of life and not words of death.

Hearing, believing, and confessing the Word is repentance toward God and faith toward the Lord Jesus Christ. Saving faith is believing that Christ died for your sins, was buried, and rose from the dead after three days in his grave.

Repentance alone does not qualify a sinner for salvation; faith is also necessary. True repentance is coupled with faith. It is impossible to have saving faith and not repent. Repentance toward God and faith toward our Lord Jesus Christ are essential and inseparable in salvation. Faith without repentance is null and the ultimate state of hypocrisy; and repentance without faith in the birth, death, burial, and resurrection of Christ is of no effect. "God desires truth in our inward parts and commands all men everywhere to repent" (Acts 17: 30). When there is true repentance, God sweeps our sins away as if they were a cloud; he blows our sins away as if they were the morning mist.

The Lord God Almighty is Lord of us all and richly blesses all who call on him. God is no respecter of persons; he loves each one of us, even you. Selah. Selah means to ponder, think about, or mediate on. God is Lord over the sinner and saint.

Jesus put on his earth suit and came to the earth to save us because we could not save ourselves from sin and its consequences. No matter how good we are, we cannot eliminate the sinful nature present in all of us. Only Jesus can do that. He did not come to help people save themselves; he came to be our Savior from the power and penalty of sin. We all are sinners, even from the moment our mothers became pregnant with us. Our sinful natures, like Judas's sinful nature, were inherited at birth.

Pray that Christ may dwell in your heart through faith to know his love, which surpasses knowledge. The love of Christ in its fullness is beyond all human comprehension; it is unknown and unknowable by the greatest minds of humankind. Yet by faith, the most humble believer can begin to know the love of Christ.

I love praying this prayer, will you pray with me? "I am grateful to you, my Lord, for your death on the cross, where the sting and shame of death was turned to eternal life, your true life. Now that I am born again, true life begins, and hopes blossom for my name to not be blotted out of the Book of Life. I will stand strong and courageous when you judge all nations and creations."

God will judge everything and every people. This includes everything, perceived or hidden. God will judge everything, whether it is good or evil. God's eye sees all, searches all, knows all, hears all, and watches all. God pronounces the end from the beginning. God knows all.

There is not a dark place or deep shadow for those who do true evil to hide. How terrible will be Day of Judgment for people who do everything they can to hide their deeds and plans from the Lord. They do their work in darkness and secret. They think, *who sees me? Who will know?* They turn everything upside down. Can what was made say to the one who made it, "You did not make me"? Can the pot say to the potter, "You do not know anything"? Nothing God created is hidden from him. His eyes see everything. He will hold us all accountable for everything we do.

Lord, you are my God. I honor you, and I worship you. I praise your name, Jesus. You are perfectly faithful and do wonderful things that were birthed long ago. You are God, and there is no other God. You are the great Jehovah, the great I AM, the God-Man. For you are the Father, the Son, and the Holy Spirit, the three who are one, the Trinity. There is no one like you, Master. Before something even happens, you announce how it will end and what is to come. Hallelujah!

God's plans always succeed. "I will do anything I want to do. I will bring about what I have said. I will do what I have planned," says the Lord. Who has made what happen? Who has carried out what? Who has created all of the people who have ever lived? God says, "I AM the Lord God and there is no change or variable in me" (James 1:17). "I was with the first of them, and I will be with the last of them. I make the sun shine by day. I order the moon and stars to shine at night. I tell the waters to come thus far, and I stir up the ocean and its waves roar. I rule over all." Suppose the sky above could be measured; suppose the foundations of the earth below could be completely discovered. "I AM the creator and sustainer of all things" (Isaiah 40:28), says the Lord.

The time is here for all things to begin to be made right. God's view of time and our view of time are different; with the Lord, a day is like a thousand years, and a thousand years are like a day. Prophecies of old are unfolding and manifesting before us every day. The time to watch, obey, and occupy is now upon us. The time is now to believe God for his insights, concepts, and ideals from heaven for earth. Selah.

"God's thoughts are not like our thoughts, nor are His ways like our ways. For as the heavens are higher than the earth, so are God's ways and thoughts higher. Before time, God was God. God's Word goes forth from His mouth, creates, and never returns void. It accomplishes what God pleases, and it prospers in the thing for which it was sent" (Isaiah 55:8-11). In choosing us, God did so before the creation of the world. What an awesome and consuming God we serve! "Oh, taste and see that the Lord is good and His mercy endures forever" (1 Chronicles 16:34, Psalm 34:8). People who are right with God live the way he wants them to live, but those who refuse to obey him trip and fall.

What did God reveal to you in chapter 1? Did you catch any new revelations?

_____
_____
_____
_____
_____
_____
_____
_____
_____
_____
_____
_____
_____
_____
_____
_____
_____
_____
_____

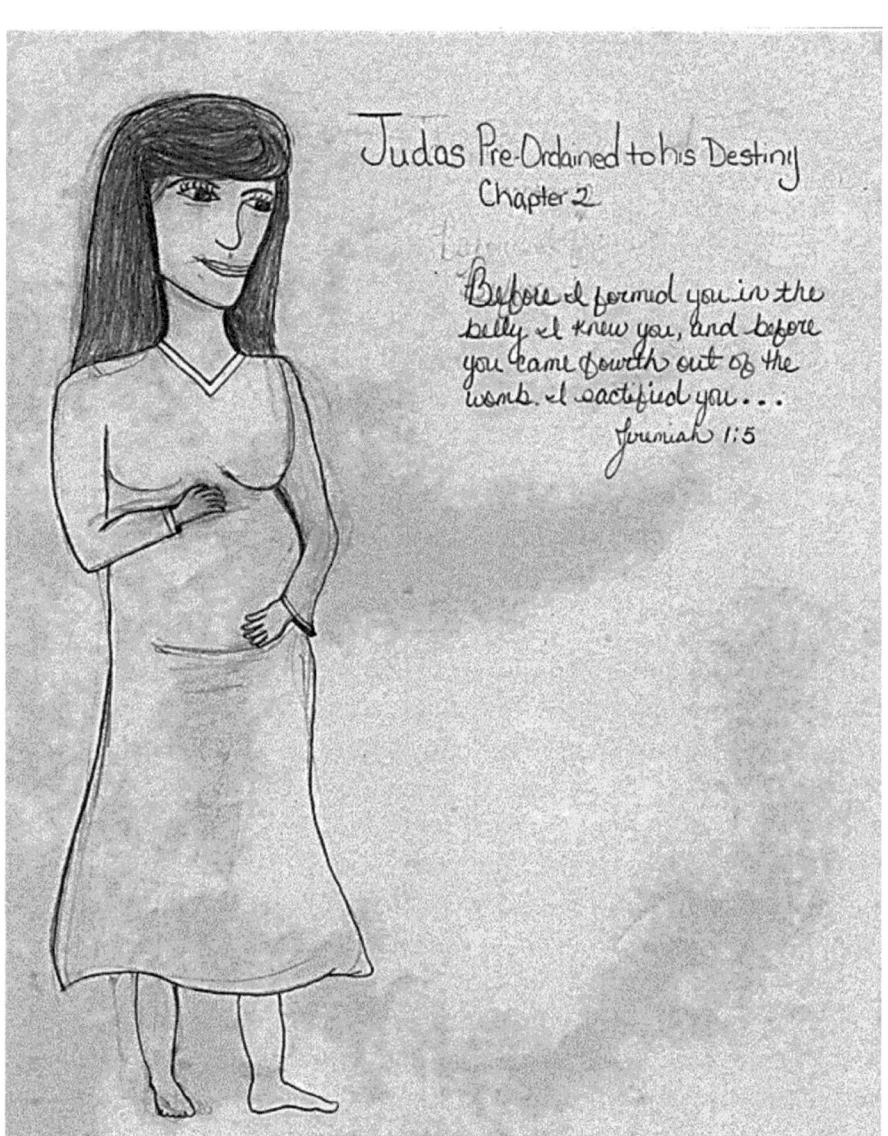

Chapter 2
JUDAS PREORDAINED TO HIS DESTINY

It took great courage to be Judas; it took strength for Judas to obey God's calling for his life and walk out his appointed destiny. God put his spirit on Judas. I believe that this is a prayer that could have been prayed by Judas, "Strengthen me, Lord, to do what you want me to do, for you are my God. May your Spirit lead me on a good path that leads to eternal life in heaven. Praise the Lord, you angels of His, praise Him, you mighty ones who carry out His orders and obey His commands. Praise the Lord, all you who serve Him and do what He ordains. Let everything the Lord has created praise Him, everything in His kingdom."

Judas's spirit answered and said, "I can do all things through Christ, who strengthens me. I praise you, Lord. I will walk out my destiny, your divine purpose and plans, and it is my gift to help redeem a lost people, your beloved."

God equipped Judas's spirit with God-given *shalom* (peace) to fulfill the gifts and calling on his life. Before Judas was born, the Lord chose him to serve him. He appointed Judas Iscariot by name and encoded in his DNA what he needed to endure his calling of betrayal. "Before I formed you in the womb, I knew you. Before you were born, I sanctified you. I ordained you a prophet to the nations, said the Lord" (Jeremiah 1:5). I believe Judas said, "I belong to God, and I will serve him. He made my words like a sharp sword. He hid me in the palm of his hand. He made me into a sharpened arrow. He takes good care of me and keeps me. I am forever the servant of the Most High God. God's glory will show through my actions, and history's record of me will be forgiveness and understanding. My God has rewarded me well, and heaven is my eternal home. The Lord formed me in my mother's body and called me out his servant. In my mother's body, God anointed my spirit. In my mother's body, God ingrained my purpose in my DNA because I was chosen to participate with the gathering of the people of Israel to God."

"For I know the thoughts that I think toward you, says the Lord, thoughts of peace and not of evil, to give you a future and a hope" (Jeremiah 29:11).

How terrible it would be for anyone to argue with his creator and sustainer. How unimaginable it would be for my spirit to argue with my creator; God is my Lord, and I am his servant. Can a piece of clay say to the potter, "Shape me into rock"? How awful it would be for anyone to say to his or her father, "Why did you give me life?" How terrible for anyone to say to his mother, "Why have you brought me out of your womb into this world?"

I believe this is a prayer that Judas would have prayed, "Lord, you are my Father. I am the clay. You are the potter. Your hands made all of us, and you only have a say. Mold me into what you must. Before you formed me inside of my mother, you had chosen me. Before I was born, you called me and set me apart to serve you."

The secret things belong to the Lord our God, but those things that are being revealed belong to us and to our children, that we may obey all the words of the law.

Everything that is secret is being brought out into the open, into the know. Everything that is hidden is being uncovered. What you have said in the dark is being revealed in the daylight. The secrets of Judas's true calling and destiny are being brought into the open, into the now. *El Roi* reveals the deep and secret things in its season. *El Roi* means the God who sees and oversees all creation and the affairs of people. God Almighty is omnipotent (all-powerful), omniscient (all knowing), and omnipresent (everywhere). God is the *alpha* and the *omega*, the all-consuming Father. God knows the end before the beginning is completed. God is God, and he always will be God. If God brings you to it, he will bring you through it.

Judas's betrayal of Jesus was his destiny. It was preordained. Jesus always knew and foresaw his betrayer; this is why Judas was chosen as one of the twelve. Jesus encouraged Judas to move swiftly in doing his act of betrayal. Without Jesus' betrayal by Judas, scriptures could not have been fulfilled, such as David foretelling of a trial and rejection (Isaiah 53:1-12, Psalm 118:22, 2 Samuel 23:3, Deuteronomy 32:4, 2 Samuel 2:31).

With his natural understanding, Judas had no way to fully understand and comprehend the enormity of his action of betraying Christ. Moreover, after the realization of his actions and those consequences, his grief and guilt were too heavy to bear, so Judas hung himself. Judas died before Christ was crucified, and I believe that his spirit was one of the spirits that Jesus presented to the Father after his resurrection where he presented God his shed blood along with the keys to death and the grave.

By walking out this destiny as the betrayer of Jesus, Judas completed the most precious act toward redemption for all humanity.

God has mercy on whom He chooses to have mercy, He has compassion on whom He chooses to have compassion, and He hardens whom He wants to harden (Romans 9:15). God's grace does not depend on man's desire or effort, but on God's mercy. For as God said to Pharaoh, "I raised you up for this very purpose, that I might display my power in you and that my name might be proclaimed in all the earth" (Exodus 9:16).

Does not the potter have the right to make out of the same lump of clay some pottery for a good purpose and some for common use? God is the self-existent creator. He has the sovereign right to do whatever pleases him. God is in charge of all people at all times.

God's foreknowledge is not like our foreknowledge. Human foreknowledge is to know or have foresight of things to come beforehand. Our foreknowledge is naturally imperfect and very fallible. With God, however, the entire course of history, in every detail, is perfectly clear and settled. This is why history is sometime called "HIStory." Selah.

God predestines nations according to his foreknowledge. He predestines individuals for service according to his foreknowledge. God is both sovereign creator (he made all things) and sustainer (he keeps all things functioning) of his creation.

Jesus is the omniscience of one who knew on the one hand the ways of his eternal Father among men, and who on the other, penetrated into the deepest recesses of human character and beheld there all its secret feelings and motives and tendencies.

God has absolute authority and right of dominion over all of His creation. He is in absolute control of all things and all people. "We know that all things work together for good to those who love God and act according to his purpose and plan" (Romans 8:28). I believe that Judas loved God, and I know God loved Judas (John 3:16).

Judas had innate business acumen and was the keeper of the purse. In the poem entitled "Judas, My Son" by John Piper, it tells of Judas as a child stealing from the offerings. The stench of Judas's greed permeated from the material to the spiritual; his greed and ambition gave way to jealousy, spite, and hatred.

Judas's new found awareness of his actions as the betrayer of Jesus led him to attempt to cast the blame of his dreadful deeds upon the chief priests and elders. He sought to redeem himself and reverse the deed by giving back the thirty pieces of silver because his guilt and shame were too heavy to carry. Then, to fulfill prophecy, Judas went and hung himself. It was a tragic end, but his death fulfilled the purpose and destiny for the one we know as Judas Iscariot, our brother in Christ.

I believe that God said to Judas, "Do not be afraid to give up the good to go for the great, Judas. Do not fear, for I AM with you. Do not be dismayed, for I AM is your God I AM will strengthen you and help you. I AM will uphold you with my righteous right hand." Judas's spirit said, "I trust you, Lord. My time is in your hands. I AM your clay. Mold me as you may."

We know that faith works best where the will of God is known or caught. God's grace, unmerited favor, and enabling ability propelled Judas's inner man to say, "I obey you, Lord.

Your will is my will."

The great I AM smiled.

What did God reveal to you in chapter 2? Did you catch any new revelations?

Peter returning Judas's corpse back to his loving father

Chapter 3
YOUNG JUDAS ISCARIOT

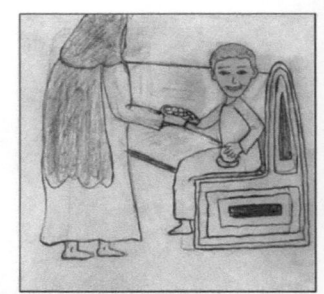

Centuries before he was born, Judas's destiny was ordained. It was inevitable. Not Judas himself nor the whole nation of the Jews, which he represented, nor all the powers of earth or heaven could keep him from betraying our Lord or from buying the Field of Blood.

"How precious are your thoughts of me; how great is the sum of all your plan and purposes" (Psalm 139:17). Judas had the right to ask, "Why bring me out of my mother's body?" He had the right to think, *I wish I had died before anyone saw me. I wish I had never been born! I wish I had been carried straight from my mother's body to the grave! Aren't my few days almost over? Leave me, so I can have a moment of joy. Turn away before I go to the place I cannot return. It is the land of darkness and deep shadow, where even the light is like darkness.* Before I was formed in the womb, Lord, you knew me. Before I was born, you sanctified me and ordained me an apostle for the generations and all nations.

Below is a beautiful and insightful poem entitled "Judas, My Son" by John Piper. John Piper pens such a vivid and realistic picture of Judas's earlier days and gives the reader some possible ideal of Judas's early days, where the Bible is silent.

> For generations without shame
> Iscariot had been a name
> In Kirioth that everyone
> Could trust, until the only son
> Of Simon came of age and broke
> His father's heart. The common folk
> Had thought it strange that Simon stayed
> Unmarried after Mary laid
> Her fevered head on Simon's chest

And died before her swollen breast

Gave one day's milk. He never told
His parents why, nor did they scold
or press him for another wife.
For thirty years, he lived his life
A widower with one great goal:
To love his son and save his soul.
No one but Simon knew what she
Had said that night. It was a plea,
And full of boding pain.
She said, "I fear, my love, that we have bred
A child of woe. And I have dreamed
A dream this night wherein it seemed
Th at something out of the abyss
Is here, and if he should but kiss,
It would mean death.
O Simon, what Have I brought forth, and we begot?
What evil deed and endless blot
Upon the name Iscariot?"
He held her in the candlelight
And fearful quietness all night.
"Dear Simon, can you see the dawn?"
"Not yet. The night is not yet gone."
"For me it is," she said, "and O,
Th at I could take the boy and go!
Or second best: that he had not
Been born! O love, no matter what
He does . . . or is, do not despair
Or sink in utter gloom, or bear
What is not yours to bear. Come near.
Th ink not that you have failed, nor fear
Th at God's unworthy of your trust
Or that in this he is unjust."
And thus she died. And Simon bowed

Above her restful face and vowed
Th at he would marry none, but give
His love as long as he might live
To show his son the path of life
And void the warnings of his wife.
For twenty-seven years he trained
His son in righteous ways, and drained
The reservoir of love and hope
So low at times he scarce could cope
With thankless days and brazen face
And haughty eyes and sore disgrace.
For years the boy stole from the offerings at
The synagogue, and once he spat
Into the Rabbi's face when he
Was caught. One time he said, "I'll be
The keeper of the king's account
Someday. You watch. And the amount
I steal from him will make this theft
Look like a petty thing." And so, bereft
Of conscience, Judas mocked the cares
And pain of Simon, and his prayers.
The young men in the village said,
"Th at Judas-boy would steal the bread
And cup right off Messiah's plate."
His father never laughed.
"It's late,
My son," he said one night. The men—
The older ones—they say, 'How can A twig,
when it is bent, grow straight?'
O Judas, Judas, it is late.
Come, make with me a brand new start,
 I love you, son, with all my heart."
For one last moment, Judas stood
And looked into his father's good
And loving eyes. Then took his sack

And headed out the door, looked back
And said, "In three years I will own
More silver than you've ever known."
And he was gone. And Simon wept
For weeks, ate nothing, seldom slept,
And almost sank in utter gloom
But for the words on Mary's tomb:
"Sink not in darkness nor despair,
Bear not what yours is not to bear:
When you have loved and lost then trust;
The ways of God are always just."
And so three years went by until
One day, out on the northern hill
Of Kirioth, a large man walked
Before an ass-drawn cart, and talked
To no one on the way. He came
And asked, "Is there a man by name
Iscariot in town?" They showed
Him where the old man lived and bode
His days alone in simple trade.
"Are you Iscariot?" he laid
The rope across his burly frame.
"I am, and who are you?" "My name
Is Peter." "Yes? What brings you down
To Kirioth? We're not a town
Th at people come from Galilee
To see; what might your business be?"
"I knew your son." Old Simon stared
In Peter's face. "I knew you cared
About your son, and so I brought
Him home for burial. I thought
It would be easier to know
Th at he had died than just to go
On wondering." The old man stood
In silence staring at the wood Cased cart.

"Is that my son?" he said.
"Yes sir." "How long has he been dead?"
"I'm not quite sure." "How did he die?"
"He hanged himself." "Do you know why?"
"The question 'Why?' has many layers,
And, Simon, some are the affairs
Of men and some of God alone.
What we should know we have been shown.
The secret things belong to God
And there are paths we dare not trod."
The old man smiled beneath his tears,
"You sound like someone many years ago."
"Yes, Simon, she spoke well.
My Master sent me here to tell
You that her dying words were true.
And I can vouch that he like you
Has wept beside the mouth of hell.
But, Simon, one is not to dwell
Forever weeping in that place
Nor contemplate the end of grace Too long.
Remember what she said,
And what you wrote when she was dead:
'Sink not in darkness, nor despair,
Bear not what is not yours to bear;
When you have loved and lost then trust,
The ways of God are always just.'"
And so the light in candle two
Cannot suffice to answer you,
If you would know before its time
The deepest "why?" of every crime.
But trust for now what it reveals;
The time will come for opened seals.

The time is now for God to reveal the hidden secret regarding Judas's destiny and his home in heaven for a time, such as it is.

God often does not give us long-term guidance about our future. His leading is more often just about the next step to take. The psalmist said to God, "Your word is a lamp to my feet and a light to my path" (Psalm 119:105). The Bible never claims to tell us about everything.

The Holy Spirit, who dwells here on the earth, reveals revelations through reading, mediating, and studying the written God-inspired Word. The Holy Spirit also tells us what He hears the Father say of us, and through our prayer time, the true fellowship-conversation, guidance, encouragement, and affirmation are given. Jesus said, "When He, the Spirit of truth, has come, He will guide you into all truth" (John 16:13). God guides through inner conviction, prayer, circumstances, and the Bible. God also guides in unexpected ways.

The Holy Spirit, the Counselor, is an inner guide to all people sent from the Father. The Spirit teaches all things and will remind you of everything that God has spoken to you.

What did God reveal to you in chapter 3? Did you catch any new revelations?

Chapter 4
THE TWELVE. THE ANOINTED DOZEN

Jesus formed his inner circle by choosing the twelve, and they were designated apostles. The twelve were Simon (whom he named Peter); his brother Andrew; James, the son of Zebedee and his brother John (to them he gave the name Boanerges, which means Sons of Th under); Philip; Bartholomew; Matthew; Thomas; James, the son of Alphaeus; Thaddaeus; Simon, who was called the Zealot; and Judas Iscariot, son of Simon. The apostle, the disciple, the man born to betray Jesus and to fulfill the scriptures prophesied by many prophets of old was one of Jesus' chosen twelve.

Long before Judas was born, King David prophesied by the spirit of God and made several very definite predictions concerning Judas. David prophesied that Judas was to acquire a piece of property, but neither he nor others were to dwell in it.

He also would have the place of an overseer; it would be taken from him and given to another.

Was it possible for Judas to avoid fulfilling these scriptures? No, Judas could not make the Word of God void or alter it. No man can make the Word of God or the plans of God void or alter it. Is it right for God to bring a man into this world with such a burden? Yes, Jesus knew when he chose Judas that Judas possessed everything he needed to fulfill the plan of betrayal for the Son of Man.

When morning had arrived, Jesus went up on the mountain side and called his twelve disciples to him, that they might be with him and that he might send them out to preach and to have authority to drive out demons. Jesus sent them out two by two. "Behold, I have given you the authority to trample on serpents and scorpions, and over all the power of the enemy, and nothing shall by any means hurt you. Nevertheless do not rejoice in this, that the spirits are subject to you, but rather rejoice because your names are written in heaven" (Luke 10:18–20). Judas went out with Peter. Weeks later, the disciples returned with joy and said, "Lord, even the demons are subject to us in Your name" (Luke 10:17). Judas and his brothers of disciples were sent out to preach the good news, the gospel, and that the kingdom of heaven was near. They fed the poor, healed the sick, raised the dead, cleansed those having leprosy, and drove out demons. "Freely you have received, freely give," Jesus told them (Matthew 10:8).

Jesus considered Judas a close friend and loved him. Jesus said of him, "Even my close friend, whom I trusted, he who shared my bread, will lift up his heel against me" (Psalm 41:9) Jesus knew well there was a destiny keeper in the camp that he chose, and he patiently kept the secret.

"Did I not choose you, the twelve? And one of you is a devil?" He spoke of Judas Iscariot, the son of Simon Iscariot (John 6:70–71). Jesus loved, protected, and kept the disciples safe so that none would be lost *except the one doomed to destruction* so that scriptures would be fulfilled and provide a path to eternal salvation for all, including Judas Iscariot, son of Simon (John 17:12).

The disciples were confused by Jesus' assertion that one of them was a devil. Do you think that any of them guessed that it was Judas? I believe Peter discerned Judas's evil and had some revelation of Judas's future. Peter also perceived Judas's destiny and heard the voice of the Lord in his spirit. As told in the poem "Judas, My Son," Peter obeyed God and returned his brother's dead corpse to his father for a proper burial and to soothe the pains of a loving father's heart.

What did God reveal to you in chapter 4? Did you catch any new revelations?

_____

_____

_____

_____

_____

_____

_____

_____

_____

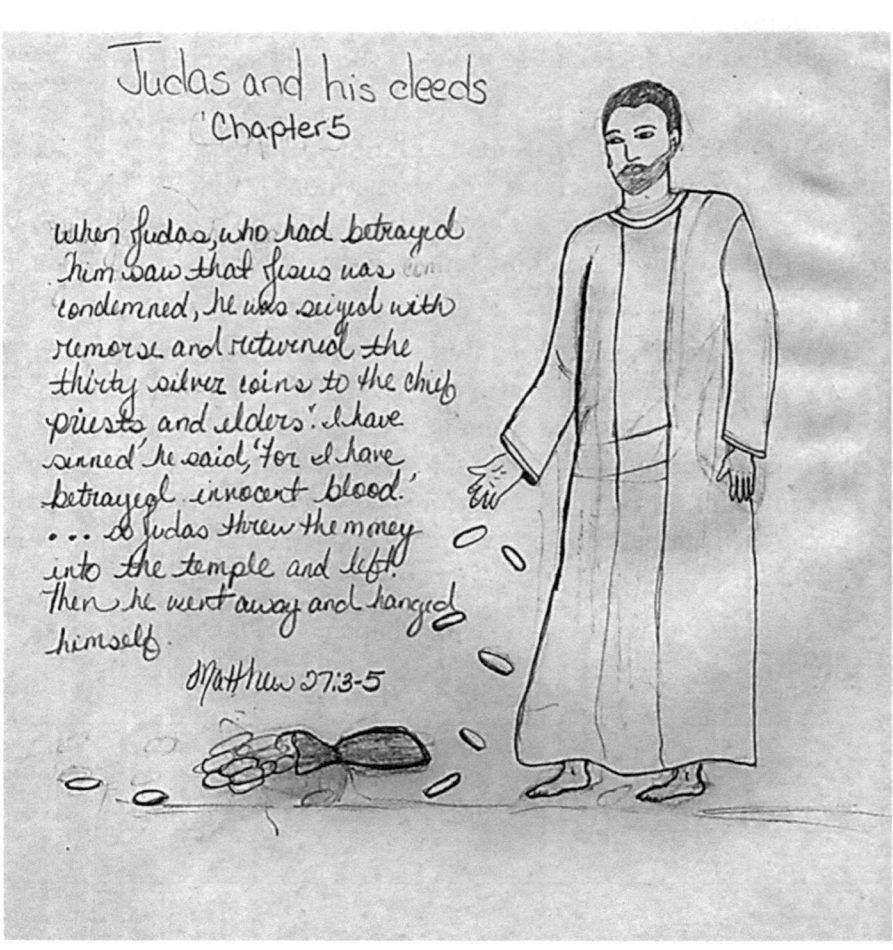

Chapter 5
JUDAS AND HIS DEEDS

Mary took a pint of pure nard, which was an expensive perfume, poured it on Jesus' feet, and wiped his feet with her hair. The fragrance permeated the house. Judas objected loudly to Mary refreshing Jesus. "'Why wasn't the perfume sold and the money given to the poor? It was worth a year's wages.' Now you know Judas did not say this because he cared about the poor but because he was a selfish man and a thief" (John 12:5–6).

Jesus told Judas to leave Mary alone, noting that her act of love and kindness was intentional and ordained out of obedience to scripture. "She has kept this for the day of My burial," he said. He then added, "For the poor you have with you from Geneses to Revelation, but Me you do not always have" (John 12:8–9).

Judas's motivation—greed and evil—was easy to see. He displayed his selfish attributes even while ministering with the other disciples, especially Peter, and in spite of seeing miracle after miracle manifested through the demonstration of the power of the spoken word and the Holy Spirit.

At the close of the third year of Christ's ministry, the chief priests and Pharisees sent their soldiers to arrest Christ, but they came back empty-handed. Their testimony showed that they had been emotionally, morally, and spiritually stunned. They reported, "No man ever spoke like this man" (John 7:46). Upon hearing Jesus for themselves and being overpowered by his words and his ethical fortitude, the temple guards had such an awe of him that they could not bring themselves to apprehend him, either as a common criminal or as a false Christ. He possessed qualities of moral integrity and divine righteousness that marked him as different from all men, including the rabbis. Indeed, they believed he was a prophet sent from God.

His claims went beyond those made by any rabbis. His teachings sparkled with truth and godliness. His holiness was unremitting, yet his compassion for the fallen was genuine and offered the forgiveness of the

Lord. His understanding of the law, even at the age of twelve, "astonished" the rabbis (Luke 2:47), who were caught in their own web of self-righteous legalism. Jesus' prayer life succeeded any major or minor prophet. He performed signs and miracles beyond those of both Elijah and Elisha, yet he called himself meek and was not boastful. Although he was a man, he was unique and set apart from all others. He alone possessed and displayed the credentials of the promised Messiah who was to come into the world.

These credentials were the outworking of his perfect moral character. He was the Messiah, and he was in the world but not of this world. His words, deeds, and manner of life authenticated his divine mission and office. Jesus knew that all things had been given into his hands and that he had come from God and went back to God. He is all-knowing regarding the destiny of everyone, including Judas.

At Passover, Jesus and the twelve went up into an upper room to rest. Jesus told Judas, the keeper of the bag, to buy the things that they needed for a feast and something to feed to the poor.

At the feast, Jesus arose to wash his hands and pull off his travel garment. He then poured water into a basin, took a towel, and humbly began to wash the tired, dusty feet of the twelve disciples. Jesus washed Judas's feet first and then moved on to the others.

Judas held a prominent place in the circle of the twelve because he was the keeper of the finances for their work and journey. It took courage for Judas to walk out his destiny, be in the presence of such anointing and be the traitor among this band of brothers. His craftiness was concealed for a time, but as time passed, his true nature was revealed for the rest of the disciples to see.

Only Jesus knew the extent of the evil powers that were at work against him. Jesus said, "I do not speak concerning all of you. I know whom I have chosen; but that the scripture may be fulfilled, He who eats bread with me has lifted up his heel against Me" (Psalm 41:9). "Now I tell you this before it comes, that when it does come to pass, you may believe that I AM HE. Most assuredly, I say to you, he who receives whomever I send receives Me: and he who receives Me receives Him who sent Me" (John 13:36). In neither instance did Jesus mention Judas by name. It seems as if Jesus was grieved for Judas and his pending deed and wished to give Judas every opportunity of repenting.

After Judas shared in the breaking of bread, Satan entered into Judas Iscariot, and he left the supper room immediately (John 13:27). Afterward, he made his compact with the chief priests. He had decided to identify Jesus by taking some troops of the chief priests to Jesus' camp. The time for his purpose and destiny was upon him. Judas knew that the Jewish leaders wanted to kill Jesus; they accused Jesus of blasphemy.

The opportunity for which he was born had come. He made his way to the high priests and their followers to collect his thirty pieces of silver and then to identify Jesus to the Roman soldiers by placing a kiss on the cheek of his Master.

"The one I kiss is Jesus," Judas told the Roman soldiers. Judas gave Christ the kiss of death on his cheek, and the soldiers gripped Jesus to take him away. In defense of Jesus, Peter raised his sword to defend Jesus and cut off the ear of one of the soldiers. Jesus, knowing that this was his "now time," told Peter to hold his peace. Jesus bent down, picked up the bleeding ear off the ground, and miraculously restored the severed ear of the soldier. The injured soldier revered that his ear was restored, that there was no blood. He understood in that moment that this man was indeed the Christ.

The Judas kiss led to Jesus' arrest, which led to a spectacle made of Jesus publicly and then to his physical crucifixion.

Judas was merely fulfilling God's plan for humanity. His betrayal was essential and necessary; he had no choice but to betray Jesus Christ, the anointed one who carried out God's plan for salvation and redemption. God's Son had to be sacrificed and then resurrected. In sacrificing one son, God gained all of the sons of the earth. Selah.

A Roman governor named Pilate tried Jesus. Pilate wanted to release Jesus, but the Jews threatened to riot, so Pilate condemned Jesus to death on the cross to fulfill the prophecy. Without Judas knowing where Jesus often gathered to fellowship and rest with his disciples, without Judas taking a band of men and officers from the chief priests and Pharisees armed with torches and weapons to capture Jesus, my beloved, the scriptures prophesied by the Holy Spirit through the mouth of David could not be fulfilled.

The soul of Jesus was an offering for our sin, for Judas's sin. He bore the sin of many and made intercession for all transgressors. He became the ultimate seed sown through which he prolongs our days, and the pleasure of the Lord prospers. "I tell you the solemn truth, *unless a kernel of wheat falls into the ground and dies, it remains by itself, alone. But if it dies, it produces much grain"* (John12:24).

Jesus was sentenced to death by crucifixion. He was beaten beyond recognition by the Roman soldiers, scourged, stripped, had part of his beard plucked out, was forced to carry his own cross, and finally was nailed to it. Our Lord was crucified between two thieves on a hill called Golgotha. He hung on the cross, bled, and died to redeem you and me from the curse of death, sin, poverty, and disease. He hung on the cross to set captives free, like Judas. He hung on cross so that you and I would not face the sting of death.

His crucified body was placed in the new tomb of a rich man named Joseph of Arimathea for burial. Jesus had promised the disciples he would come back three days after he died. Knowing the rumors of resurrection, the Roman governor placed soldiers at the tomb of Jesus to prevent his body from being stolen and Jesus' resurrection fabricated.

Christ's crucifixion was a part of God's plan of salvation. Jesus was slain on the cross for the salvation of all the beloved. He did not attempt to avoid the cross because he knew it as the will of the Father to be crucified, to pay for sins of the beloved, and to give salvation to believers throughout the ages. Jesus knew that he came to earth as the God-Man to die on the cross. He said that, "He is the Good Shepherd and that no one takes His life; He gives it freely" (John 10:11).

To be offered up and crucified, "Jesus had to be despised and rejected by men. He became a man of sorrows who was acquainted with grief. Jesus bore our grief and carried our sorrows by being stricken, smitten by God, and afflicted. He was wounded for our transgressions, he was bruised for our iniquities; the chastisement for our peace was upon him, and by his stripes we are all healed. He was oppressed and He was afflicted, yet He opened not his mouth. He was led as a lamb to the slaughter but did not mumble a word. For the transgressions of us all, He was stricken. Yet it pleased the Lord to bruise him" (Isaiah 53:38).

While in the grave, Jesus uttered this prayer of despondency Psalm 88:

O Lord, God of my salvation,
I have cried out day and night before You.
Let my prayer come before You; incline
Your ear to my cry. For my soul is full of troubles,

and my life draws near to the grave.
I am counted with those who go down to the pit;
I am like a man who has no strength,
adrift among the dead, like the slain who lie in the grave,
 whom You remember no more,
and who are cut off from Your hand.
You have laid me in the lowest pit, in darkness,
in the depths. Your wrath lies heavy upon me,
and You have afflicted me with all Your waves. Selah.
You have put away my acquaintances far from me;
You have made me an abomination to them;
I am shut up, and I cannot get out;
my eye wastes away because of affliction.
Lord, I have called daily upon You;
I have stretched out my hands to You.
Will You work wonders for the dead?
Shall the dead arise and praise You? Selah.
Shall Your lovingkindness be declared in the grave?
Or Your faithfulness in the place of destruction?
Shall Your wonders be known in the dark?
And Your righteousness in the land of forgetfulness?
But to You I have cried out, O Lord,
And in the morning my prayers comes before You.
Lord, why do You cast off my soul?
Why do You hide Your face from me?
I have been afflicted and ready to die from my youth;
I suffer Your terrors; I am distraught.
Your fierce wrath has gone over me;
Your terrors have cut me off.
They came around me all day long like water;
they engulfed me   altogether.
Loved one and friend You have put far from me,
and my acquaintances into darkness. (Psalm 88:1–18)

New Birth Announcement:

After spending three days in the grave, Jesus arose, then He ascended to heaven to deliver His purity and the keys of death, hell, and the grave to the Father. Jesus reopened the path for sinful humans to regain what Adam lost in the Garden of Eden (John 11:23).

The kingdom of God is seedtime and harvest time. While the earth remains, seedtime and harvest, cold and heat, winter and summer, and day and night shall not cease. Through Jesus' death on the cross, God sowed his son, Jesus, as a seed to reap a harvest of all sons and daughters.

I have ransomed you from the power of the grave; I have redeemed You from death: O death, I AM thy plagues; O grave, I AM thy destruction: repentance is hidden from mine eyes (Hosea 13:14).

Jesus is the resurrection and the life (John 11:25–26). After His resurrection, He commanded believers to go and preach the gospel (Matthew 28:19–20). The name of Jesus is above every name in all creation. Preaching of the Gospel is called preaching the Good News, simply stated, God's all-consuming love for us and his ultimate saving power.

What did God reveal to you in chapter 5? Did you catch any new revelations?

_____

_____

_____

_____

_____

_____

_____

_____

_____

The Gates to Eternal Life

Chapter 6
JUDAS IS IN HEAVEN

"Sing, O heavens, for the Lord has done it! Shout, you lower parts of the earth; break forth into singing, your mountains, O forest, and every tree in it! For the Lord has redeemed Jacob, and glorified Himself in Israel" (Isaiah 44:23).

By ascending to heaven with the keys of death, hell, and the grave, Jesus led captives from the belly of hell into heaven, our holy dwelling place. Notwithstanding in this rejoice not, that the spirits are subject unto you; but rather rejoice, because your names are written in heaven. This was told to the twelve disciples by Jesus (Luke 10:20).

Jesus was the author and the developer of Judas's faith. God did not give Judas the spirit of fear but power to be self-centered and greedy. If you grow weak when trouble comes, your strength is very small.

"Son of man, do not be afraid of them nor be afraid of their words, though briers and thorns are with you and you dwell among scorpions; do not be afraid of their words or dismayed by their looks, though they are a rebellious house. You shall speak My words to them, whether they hear or whether they refuse, for they are rebellious. But you, son of man, hear what I say to you. Do not be rebellious like that rebellious house; open your mouth and eat what I give you" (Ezekiel 2:6–8).

This is what the Lord said to Ezekiel when he chose him to have courage to face adverse circumstances. I believe that if more had been revealed about Judas's calling, it would have read the same.

"Judas, my child, woven in your DNA is courage to face adverse circumstances and faith to walk through a destiny no other can. Judas, my child, woven in your DNA is strength to face adverse circumstances and faith to walk through a destiny no other can. Judas, my child, woven in your DNA is *shalom* peace to face adverse circumstances and faith to walk through a destiny no other can. Selah.

"Judas, my child, if you stand firm you will gain eternal, glorious life. Judas, my child, your life and act of betrayal help ransom my people by becoming a bridge for Jesus to be crucified and then resurrected."

I imagine Judas would have responded, "I only want to finish my race, complete my purpose." Judas accepted his appointment with his destiny and said, "It shall be, so it is. I AM a destiny keeper, and my reward is heaven." Selah.

We must remember the words of the Lord Jesus, who said, "It is more blessed to give than to receive" (Acts 20:35). Judas gave himself back to God. He was remorseful; the condemnation of Jesus had awakened Judas's sense of guilt. Growing more despondent and repulsed at the chief priests and elders, Judas repented, declared Jesus innocent, and confessed his sin. He threw down the pieces of silver in the temple, left, and went away and hanged himself (Matthew 27:3–5). When Judas hung himself, he committed himself back into God's care. Death does not separate us from the love or hand of God. Nothing can separate us from Christ's love—not death nor life, not angels nor demons, not the present, the future, nor any powers—because of what Christ Jesus our Lord has done for us through the cross. Nothing but sin separates us from God (Romans 8:38–39). Repent of your sin and enjoy the presence of God.

"'I have sinned, for I have betrayed innocent blood,' said Judas. He threw the silver to the ground and left." (Matthew 27:4-5).

Not knowing what to do with the blood money that Judas had thrown down, the chief priests purchased the potter's field to fulfill that which was spoken by Jeremiah the prophet, called the Field of Blood (Matthew 27:8). This piece of land was purchased with the money Judas received for betraying Jesus. It is written that Judas fell over in this field in such a way that his intestines burst out, and he died. This would imply that the name refers to the blood of Judas. The clay also had a strong red color, which may be the origin of the modern name (Jeremiah 19:1-2, Matthew 27:1-10).

God chose us to belong to Christ long before he created the world. He chose us to be holy and without blame in his eyes. God loves us; we are his children. It pleased God for Jesus to die on the cross, which brought praise to God's glorious grace. God freely gave us his grace and mercy because he loves us.

Judas's soul was set free because of Christ's redemptive bloodshed on the cross. Through Jesus' shed blood, our sins has been forgiven and washed away. Judas's sins have been forgiven and washed away too.

God's grace and rich mercy have set us free. God poured his grace on us by giving us great wisdom and understanding. He showed us the mystery of his plan. It was in keeping with what he wanted to do. It was what he had planned through Christ. All of God's plans will be revealed when "HIStory" comes full circle.

God will then bring together all things in heaven and on earth under one ruler, Jesus Christ. God works out everything to fit and complete his plan and purpose. If the Lord is pleased with us, he will lead us into that land that has plenty of milk and honey. Selah.

What did God reveal to you in chapter 6? Did you catch any new revelations?

_____
_____
_____
_____
_____
_____
_____
_____
_____
_____
_____
_____
_____
_____
_____
_____
_____
_____
_____

Chapter 7
THE REVELATION OF SECRET THINGS

God keeps certain things hidden and makes them known to his children, his beloved, in his time. He does this so we can obey all of the words of this law and know all things needed to accomplish our destiny. He tells people the secrets of darkness. He brings evil plans out into the light. All that is hidden will be seen, and what is out of sight will be brought into the open and made known.

The secret of the Lord is with those who reverence him. Do you reverence him? If so, he will show you his covenant so that you can discern the secrets of his wisdom, for this will double your prudence. Can you search out the deep things of God? Has God revealed to you some of the secret things? Is it time for God to reveal your secrets? Can you imagine the limits of the Almighty? God's thoughts are higher than heaven—what can you do? Deeper than Sheol—what can you know?

God's measure is longer than the earth and broader than the sea. If God passes by, imprisons, and gathers to judgment, then who can hinder him? Here on earth, we see only in part and know only in part. We see and know only what God allows. God knows the secrets of all hearts, and he is revealing his divine secrets to all, for the time of such revelations is now.

Divine secrets are being revealed to you even while reading this book. "Oh, taste and see that the Lord is good," (Psalm 34:8). His mercy endures forever. The seals have been broken, and the shift is taking place. The day of God judging the secrets of men by Jesus Christ is at hand. The time is near for all men to fall on their face and worship our creator. God wants truth to be in each of our hearts; he teaches us wisdom deep down inside.

Jesus' birthplace was kept a secret from King Herod to protect the life and legacy of the baby Jesus so that the prophecies foretold of his birth, death, and resurrection could be fulfilled.

"The Word of God is living, moving, and sharper than any sword that has two edges. It judges the thoughts and purposes of the heart. Nothing God created is hidden from him. His eyes see everything. He holds us.accountable for everything we do and everything we say" (Hebrews 4: 12-13). Let God work in you; he wants your plans and your acts to be in keeping with his good purpose, for your good purpose.

Why Judas Was Born to Betray Jesus

I will open my mouth and tell stories. I have chosen him to walk out this very walk. I have chosen him to carry this very heavy rock, Jesus said about Judas.

I have chosen him to walk in this dark, lonely walk. I have chosen him to help bring salvation, the redemption plan, and its purpose to light. Praise God, I have chosen him, and he obeyed. Judas, I chose you, and you obeyed.

He now shows us the mystery of his plan. It was in keeping with what he wanted to do. It was what he had planned through Judas. It was what he had planned through Jesus Christ.

God decided to choose us long ago in keeping with his plan, and he works out everything to fit his plan and purpose. We were chosen to bring praise to his glory. We were chosen to serve and revere the Lord Jesus, our Christ.

We love you, Lord, although you loved us first. The Lord knows what is in our heart; he know all about us. He knows when we sit down and when we get up. He knows what we are thinking. He knows when we go out to work and when we come back home. He knows exactly how we live. Lord, even before we speak a word, You know all about it. He is all around us. He is behind us and in front of us. He holds us in his power. I am amazed at how well God knows us all. It is more than I can understand.

How can I get away from your Spirit? Where can I go to escape from you? If I go up to the heavens, you are there. If I lie down in the deepest parts of the earth, you are also there.

I love you, Lord.

Suppose I were to rise with the sun in the east and then cross over to the west, where it sinks into the ocean. Your hand would always be there to guide me. Your right hand would still be holding me close. Suppose I were to say, "I am sure the darkness will hide me. The light around me will become as dark as night." Even that darkness would shine like the day, because darkness is like light to you.

You created the deepest parts of my being. You put me together inside my mother's body. How you made me is amazing and wonderful, and I praise you for that. I love you, Lord. What you have done is wonderful, and I know that very well. None of my bones were hidden from you when you made me inside my mother's body; that place was as dark as the deepest parts of the earth. When you were knitting me together there, your eyes saw my body even before it was formed.

You planned how many days I would live. You wrote down the numbers of them in your Book of Life before I had lived through even one of them. I love you, Lord.

God, your thoughts about me are priceless. No one can possibly add them all up. If I could count them, they would be more than the grains of sand. If I were to fall asleep counting and then wake up, you would still be there with me.

Do not be naive, a bird can fly away and carry your words and report what you said. If you grow weak when trouble comes, your strength is very small. Son of man, do not be afraid of them or of what they say. Do not be afraid, even if thorns and bushes are all around you and you live among scorpions.

Do not be afraid of what they say. Do not be terrified by them. They always refuse to obey Me. You must give them my message.

They might listen, or they might not. After all, they refuse to obey Me. Son of man, listen to what I tell you. Do not be like those who refuse to obey.

"Call to Me, and I will answer you, and show you great and mighty things, which you do not know" (Jeremiah 33:3). Do not be afraid to give up the good to go for the great. So do not fear, for I AM with you. Do not be dismayed, for I AM your God. I strengthen you and help you. I will uphold you with my righteous right hand.

What did God reveal to you in chapter 7? Did you catch any new revelations?

Chapter 8
JESUS

"I will ransom [you] from the power of the grave; I will redeem [you] from death. O Death, I will be your plagues! O Grave, I will be your destruction. Pity is hidden from My eyes" (Hosea 13:14).

Unto us, a child is born—the virgin birth (Isaiah 7:14), unto us a son is given—God gave his son by adoption to Joseph and to us on the cross.

The angelic hosts are sons of God by creation; believers are sons of God by adoption.

Jesus Christ is the Son of God by his eternal relationship to God the Father.

"For unto us a Child is born, unto us a Son is given; and the government will be upon His shoulder. And his name will be called Wonderful, Counselor, Mighty God, Everlasting Father, Prince of Peace" (Isaiah 9:6). Isaiah foretold of the birth of Jesus and the reason for his birth at least five hundred years before it happened.

The birth of Jesus Christ is in direct fulfillment of many Bible prophecies. For example, Isaiah 7:14 foretold the virgin birth. Genesis 3:15 said that he would be born of the seed of woman. Isaiah 11:1 predicted that he would descend from the line of Jesse, father of King David. Micah 5:2 prophesied that he would be born in Bethlehem. Jeremiah 31:15 foretold that Herod would slaughter all the children in an attempt for the devil to kill the Christ child.

An old man named Simeon was looking for the promise consolation of Israel. The Consolation of Israel was a name for the Messiah in common use among the Jews in the Old Testament. Simeon was a righteous and devout man who lived in Jerusalem. It had been revealed to Simeon that he would not die before he had seen the Messiah, the Lord's Christ. Anna, a prophetess and of old age, worshipped and fasted to behold with her eyes the promised

Messiah. She recognized Jesus as the redeemer of Jerusalem when she saw the infant baby Jesus, who was brought to the temple at eight days of age. Simeon was moved by the Spirit to come also, and he recognized the child and took him into his arms and blessed God.

More than two thousand years ago, God sent the angel Gabriel to Nazareth to a virgin named Mary. She was engaged to Joseph, a local carpenter. Gabriel announced to Mary her impending pregnancy. He declared, "And behold, you will conceive in your womb and bring forth a Son, and shall call His name Jesus. He will be great, and will be called the Son of the Highest; and the Lord God will give Him the throne of His father David. And He will reign over the house of Jacob forever, and His Kingdom there will be no end" (Luke 1:31–33). The angel told Mary that by God's power, she would conceive and bear this son.

The virgin birth made possible the incarnation, meaning God became flesh and dwelt among us. Jesus pre-existed before his birth into humanity. God became a man with human infirmity and emptied himself of the glory of heaven in order that he might take upon himself the sins, diseases, and weaknesses of our humanity. Jesus was born to redeem humanity from the curses of this world. He was the One in which both full divinity and full humanity was present, distinct, and unique. Mary, highly favored by the Lord and surely confused, maybe even frightened, who had not known a man intimately, was engaged to be married; and having inspired faith in God, she replied, "Let it be to me according to your word" (Luke 1:38).

When Joseph learned that Mary was pregnant, an angel had to appear to Joseph in a dream to explain to him the wonderful reason why his virgin wife was pregnant. The angel told Joseph not to be afraid to take Mary as his wife, for that which was begotten in her was by the Holy Spirit. Mary had supernaturally conceived, and she would give birth to a son, whom Joseph must call Jesus, for he would save all people from their sins. Joseph, inspired by faith in God, said, "Father, your will is my will." Angels are ministering spirits of the Lord sent forth to minister to and for us.

The name *Jesus* in Hebrew means, "Jehovah is Salvation." The sinless nature of Jesus was not because of the virgin birth but because of Jesus' eternal relationship with God the Father. Jesus is eternally sinless. He is the God who became a man, then shed his earth suit and now abides in heaven.

Birth Announcement:

"For there is born to you this day in the city of David a Savior, who is Christ the Lord. And this will be the sign to you: You will find a Babe wrapped in swaddling clothes, lying in a manger" (Luke 2:11–12).

Joseph took his pregnant wife to Bethlehem to register for a census for taxation. In Bethlehem, there were no rooms available at the inn; so, to fulfill prophecy, Mary gave birth to Jesus in a stable where the animals slept. Shepherds and wise men following a divine star visited the baby Jesus, fell down, and worshipped him. These men opened their treasures, presenting gifts of gold and frankincense and myrrh to honor the baby Jesus.

Jesus came into the world to buy back through atonement what Adam lost. "Behold! The Lamb of God, who takes away the sin of the world!" (John 1:29). Jesus is the Word who became flesh and dwelled among us. Th rough Jesus' redemption of humanity from sin, we regain the nature that God had intended with the creation of the first man, Adam. Jesus was unique in his person, in his birth, in his ministry, in his death, in his resurrection, and in his ascension, and he will be unique in his second coming. "No one knows about the day nor hour, not even the angels in heaven, nor the Son, but only the Father. As were the days of Noah, so shall be the coming of the Son of man. For as in those days which were before the flood they were eating and drinking, marrying and giving in marriage, until the day that Noah entered into the ark, and they knew not until the flood came, and took them all away; so shall be the coming of the Son of man. Then shall two man be in the fi eld; one is taken, and one is left: two women shall be grinding at the mill; one is taken, and one is left. Watch therefore: for ye know not on what day your Lord cometh. But know this, that if the master of the house had known in what watch the thief was coming, he would have watched, and would not have suffered from his house being broken into.

Therefore, be ye also ready; for in an hour that ye think not the Son of man cometh.

Who then is the faithful and wise servant, whom his lord hath set over his household, to give them their food in due season? Blessed is that servant, when the lord comes, and find him doing so. Verily I say unto you, that he will set him over all that he hath. But if that evil servant shall say in his heart,

My lord tarrieth; and shall begin to beat his fellow-servants, and shall eat and drink with the drunken; the lord of that servant shall come in a day when he expecteth not, and in an hour when he knoweth not" (Matthew 24:36-50, 1 Corinthians 15:12-58). The second coming of Christ will be unmistakable, swift and sudden (Matthew 24:24-28, Matthew 24:40-42).

Jesus grew into a man to fulfill the plan of salvation. He grew up to be the advocate, the intercessor, the one mediator between man and God. He grew up so that he could die, thereby offering a perfect, sinless life in sacrifice for our sins.

Jesus was resurrected from the dead, conquering death and providing a living hope of eternal life for all who come to him. He grew up so that he might become to all those who obey him the source of eternal salvation. Jesus is the ultimate seed sown. While the earth remains, there will always be seedtime and harvest, cold and heat, winter and summer, and day and night shall not cease.

Jesus' deity is revealed in his performance of the following seven miracles so that we all might believe that he is the Christ, the Son of God; and in that believing, we may have eternal life in his name:

1. Jesus turned water into wine, proving his deity in his power to create (John 2).

2. Jesus healed the nobleman's son, proving his deity in his power to prolong life (John 4).

3. Jesus healed a sick man at the pool of Bethesda, proving his deity in his power to supply the necessities of life (John 5).

4. Jesus fed five thousand with a lad's lunch of two fishes and a loaf of bread, proving his deity in his power to supply the necessities of life (John 6).

5. Jesus walked on the water, proving his deity in his power to protect life (John 6).

6. Jesus gave sight to a blind beggar, proving his deity in his power to illuminate life (John 9).

7. Jesus raised Lazarus from the dead, proving his deity in his power to re-create life (John 11).

Although Jesus is God who came to this earth in the flesh, he was still a man who took on humankind; Jesus thirsted, hungered, felt pain and sorrow. In the garden of Gethsemane, Jesus said, "'Father, if thou be willing, remove this cup from me; nevertheless, not my will, but your will be done.' And there appeared an angel unto him from heaven, strengthening him. And being in agony he prayed more earnestly; and his sweat was as it were great drops of blood falling down to the ground" (Luke 22:42-44).

Judas did his part, so that Jesus could do his part. Selah.

Are you doing your part?

The Psalms of Jesus Lamenting

Jesus' Prayer of Being Forsaken, Psalm 69:1–21
Save me, O God!
For the waters have come up to my neck.
I sink in deep mire,
Where there is no standing; I have come into deep waters,
Where the floods overflow me.
I am weary with my crying;
My throat is dry,
My eyes fail while I wait for my God.
Those who hate me without a cause
Are more than the hairs of my head;
They are mighty who would destroy me,
Being my enemies wrongfully; Though I have stolen nothing.
I still must restore it.
O God, You know my foolishness;
And my sins are not hidden from You,
Let not those who wait for You, O Lord GOD of hosts,
be ashamed because of me;
Let not those who seek You be confounded because of me, O God of Israel.

Because for Your sake I have borne reproach; Shame has covered my face.
I have become a stranger to my brothers,
And an alien to my mother's children;
Because zeal for Your house has eaten me up,
And the reproaches of those who reproach You have fallen upon me.
When I wept and chastened my soul with fasting,
That became my reproach. I also made sackcloth my garment;
I became a byword to them.
Those who sit in the gate speak against me,
And I am the song of the drunkards.
But as for me, my prayer is to You,
O Lord, in the acceptable time; O God,
in the multitude of Your mercy, Hear me,
in the truth of Your salvation.
Deliver me out of the mire,
And let me not sink;
Let me be delivered from those who hate me,
And out of the deep waters.
Let not the floodwater overflow me,
Nor let the deep swallow me up;
And let not the pit shut its mouth on me.
Hear me, O Lord; for Your loving kindness is good;
Turn to me according to the multitude of Your tender mercies.
And do not hide Your face from Your servant,
For I am in trouble; Hear me speedily.
Draw near to my soul, and redeem it;
Deliver me because of my enemies.
You know my reproach, my shame, and my dishonor;
My adversaries are all before You.
Reproach has broken my heart,
And I am full of heaviness;
I looked for someone to take pity, but there was none;
And for comforters, but I found none.
They also gave me gall for my food,
And for my thirst they gave me vinegar to drink.

Jesus' Prayer on Being Crucified, Psalm 22:1–31
My God, My God, why have You forsaken Me?
Why are You so far from helping Me,
And from the words of my groaning?
O My God, I cry in the daytime, but You do not hear;
And in the night season, and am not silent.
But You are holy,
Who inhabit the praises of Israel.
Our fathers trusted in You;
They trusted, and You delivered them.
They cried to You, and were delivered;
They trusted in You, and were not ashamed.
But I am a worm, and no man;
A reproach of men, and despised of the people.
All those who see Me laugh Me to scorn:
They shoot out the lip, they shake the head, saying,
"He trusted in the Lord, let Him rescue Him;
Let Him deliver Him, since He delights in Him!"
But You are He who took Me out of the womb;
You made Me trust when I was on My mother's breasts.
I was cast upon You from birth.
From My mother's womb You have been My God.
Be not far from Me;
For trouble is near;
For there is none to help.
Many bulls have surrounded Me;
Strong bulls of Bashan have encircled Me.
They gape at Me with their mouths,
As a raging and roaring lion
I am poured out like water,
And all My bones are out of joint;
My heart is like wax;
It has melted within Me. My strength is dried up like a potsherd,
And My tongue clings to My jaws;
You have brought Me to the dust of death.

For dogs have surrounded Me;
The assembly of the wicked has enclosed Me.
They pierced My hands and My feet; I can count all My bones.
They look and stare at Me.
They divide My garments among them, And for My clothing they cast lots.
But You, O Lord, do not be far from Me; O My Strength, hasten to help Me!
Deliver Me from the sword,
My precious life from the power of the dog.
Save Me from the lion's mouth And from the horns of the wild oxen!
You have answered Me.
I will declare Your name to My brethren;
In the midst of the congregation I will praise You.
You who fear the Lord, praise Him! All you descendants of Jacob, glorify Him, And fear Him, all you off spring of Israel!
For He has not despised nor abhorred the affliction of the afflicted;
Nor has He hidden His face from Him; But when He cried to Him, He heard.
My praise shall be of You in the great congregation; I will pay My vows before those who fear Him.
The poor shall eat and be satisfied; Those who seek Him will praise the Lord.
Let your heart live forever!
All the ends of the world
Shall remember and turn to the Lord,
And all the families of the nations Shall worship before You. For the kingdom is the Lord's, And He rules over the nations.
All the prosperous of the earth
Shall eat and worship;
All those who go down to the dust
Shall bow before Him,
Even he who cannot keep himself alive.
A posterity shall serve him.
It will be recounted of the Lord to the next generation,
They will come and declare His righteousness to a people who will be born,
Th at He has done this.
Jesus Resurrected, Psalm 16:1–11
Preserve me, O God, for in You I put my trust.

O my soul, you have said to the Lord,
"You are my Lord,
My goodness is nothing apart from You"—
And to the saints who are on the earth,
"They are the excellent ones, in whom is all my delight."
Their sorrows shall be multiplied who hasten after another god;
Their drink offerings of blood I will not offer,
Nor take up their names on my lips.
You, O Lord, are the portion of my inheritance and my cup;
You maintain my lot.
The lines have fallen to me in pleasant places; Yes, I have a good inheritance.
I will bless the Lord who has given me counsel; My heart also instructs me in the night seasons.
I have set the Lord always before me;
Because He is at my right hand I shall not be moved.
Therefore my heart is glad, and my glory rejoices; My flesh also will rest in hope.
For You will not leave my soul in Sheol,
Nor will You allow Your Holy One to see corruption.
You will show me the path of life;
In Your presence is fullness of joy;
At your right hand are pleasures forevermore.
Jesus, King of Kings, Psalm 2:1–11
Why do the nations rage,
And the people plot a vain thing?
The kings of the earth set themselves,
And the rulers take counsel together,
Against the Lord and against His Anointed, saying,
"Let us break Their bonds in pieces
And cast away Their cords from us."
He who sits in the heavens shall laugh; The Lord shall hold them in derision.
Then He shall speak to them in His wrath, And distress them in His deep displeasure:
"Yet I have set My King
On My holy hill of Zion." "I will declare the decree:

The Lord has said to Me,
'You are My Son,
Today I have begotten You.
Ask of Me, and I will give You
The nations for Your inheritance,
And the ends of the earth for Your possession.
You shall break them with a rod of iron;
You shall dash them in pieces like a potter's vessel.'"
Now therefore, be wise, O kings;
Be instructed, you judges of the earth.
Serve the Lord with fear,
And rejoice with trembling.

Jesus ascends to Heaven, again, after spending forty days on earth fellowshipping with his disciples. When Jesus' time of Departure had come again, his disciple were sad to say goodbye. Jesus said to his disciple,

> "And I will pray the Father, and He will give you another Helper, that He may abide with you forever" while on this earth to take the place of me. The Helper will abide with you forever and will be in you and teach you all things, and bring to your remembrance all things, says Jesus (John 14:16). The Holy Spirit will convict of sin, of righteousness, and of judgment (John 16:8).
> He will guide you into all truth. He will show you things to come. He will glorify God. He will take the things of Christ and show it to you. He will guide you into all truths; for he will not speak on his authority, but whatever he hears, he will speak" (John 16:13).
>   Thank you Father for your Holy Spirit.

What did God reveal to you in chapter 8? Did you catch any new revelations?

Chapter 9
THE CHRISTIAN LIFE IS A SUCCESSFUL LIFE

We should all know God's Word, confess God's Word, meditate on God's Word, and apply God's Word for the benefit of our daily living. "Obedience is better than sacrifice" (1 Samuel 15:22). Thank you, Judas, for your obedience and sacrifice. We all now can live a successful Christian life, if we choose. As stated in Isaiah 1:19, that if we are willing and obedient, we would eat the best from the land.

"All Scripture is given by inspiration of God, and is profitable for doctrine, for reproof, correction, for instruction in righteousness," and for our edification (2 Timothy 3:16).

"This Book of the Law shall not depart from your mouth, but you shall meditate in it day and night, that you may observe to do according to all that is written. For then you will make you way prosperous and then you will have good success. Have I not commanded you? Be strong and of good courage, do not be afraid, nor be dismayed, for the Lord your God is with you wherever you go" (Joshua 1:8–9).

"God promised to supply all our needs, wants and usages" (Philippians 4:19). "God promised to open the windows of heaven and pour out a blessing so big that there will not be room enough to receive it" (Malachi 3:10). God promised to bless you in your spiritual and material need. "Give and it will be given to you: good measure, pressed down, shaken together, and running over will be put into your bosom. For with the same measure that you use, it will be measure back to you" (Luke 6:38). As you place God first in your life, he will supply all of your needs, wants, and usage. Usage means material things needed to live a productive life here on earth.

God's prayer for his children is, "Beloved (Child of God), I will, I wish, I pray that you may prosper in all things and be in health, just as your soul prospers" (3 John 1:2).

Prosperity is having the ability to meet the needs of humanity. God empowers people to prosper.

Blessing becomes an instrument through which God flows favors through you into someone else's life to prevent misfortune and provide channels for them to do the same.

What did God reveal to you in chapter 9? Did you catch any new revelations?

Chapter 10
GOD'S TIMING

Everything happens at God's appointed time, his "now time."

There is a time for everything that is done on earth, as Ecclesiastes, chapter 3 makes clear. There is a time to be born. There is a time to die. There is a time to plant. There is a time to pull up what has been planted. There is a time to kill. There is a time to heal. There is a time to tear down. There is a time to build up. There is a time to cry. There is a time to laugh. There is a time to be sad. There is a time to dance. There is a time to scatter stones. There is a time to gather them. There is a time to hug. There is a time not to hug. There is a time to search, and there is a time to stop searching.

There is a time to keep. There is a time to throw away. There is a time to fear. There is a time for rest. There is a time to mend. There is a time to break. There is a time to be silent. There is a time to speak. There is a time to hate. There is a time for war, and there is a time for peace.

What does the worker get for his hard work? God has put a heavy load on men, but he has also made everything beautiful in its time.

God also has given humanity a sense of what he has been doing down through the ages. It is not for us to figure out what he has done from the beginning to the end; we should focus on being happy, doing well, and living a decent and orderly life. God calls this "occupying until death or the resurrection, whichever one is first for you." I know that everything God does lasts forever. Everything that now exists, has always existed, has already been, and what is coming has existed before.

Everything God created looks forward to the time when his children will appear in their full and final glory. What we are suffering now is nothing compared with the glory that will be shown through us and in us.

This created world was bound to fail, not because of it own choice, but because it was planned that way by the One who made it. God planned to set the created world free. He did not want it to rot away completely. Instead, he wanted it to have the same glorious freedom that his children have. "We know that all that God created has been groaning in pain as if it were giving birth to a child" (Romans 8:22).

Remember, we have the Holy Spirit as the promise for future blessing. The Spirit groans inside us as we look forward to the time when God will adopt us as full members of his family, when he will give us everything he has for us. In death, he will raise our bodies and make them glorified. This is the hope we have when we are saved and the hope we carry every day. Hope that can be seen is no hope at all. Who hopes for what he already has? We hope for what we do not have yet. "Lord, help us to be patient as we wait for your manifestations. In the same way, the Holy Spirit helps us when we are weak" (2 Corinthians 12:10).

When we do not know what we should pray for, the Spirit himself prays for us. He prays with groans too deep for words. God, who looks into our hearts, knows the mind of the Spirit. The Spirit prays for God's people just as God wants him to pray.

Jesus could not die before his time. At the appointed time, Christ died for all ungodly people. He died for us when we had no power of our own. It is unusual for anyone to die for a godly person. Maybe someone would be willing to die for a good person, but this is how God has shown his love for us. While we were still sinners, Christ died for us (Romans 5:6–8).

The blood of Christ has made us right with God. The shed blood of Jesus ransomed Judas back to God and provided the path for Judas to spend eternity in Heaven. Once, we were God's enemies; but now, we are brought back to him because his son has died for us. Now that God has brought us back, we are even more secure. We know that we are indeed saved because Christ lives. We are full of joy in God because of our Lord Jesus Christ. Because of Jesus' sacrifice, God has brought us back to himself.

Thank you, Lord, for creating the heavens and the earth. You are God. You formed the earth and established it. You set it firmly in its place. You did not create it to be empty. Instead, you formed it for your beloved to live on. You are the Lord, and there is no other God.

Jesus said, "I AM coming quickly, and My reward is with Me, to give to everyone according to his work. I AM the Alpha and the Omega, the Beginning and the End, the First and the Last" (Revelation 22:12–13).

God's time of the great reveal is now. The fullness of time is now. Creation's shift has taken place. Selah.

What did God reveal to you in chapter 10? Did you catch any new revelations?

_____
_____
_____
_____
_____
_____
_____
_____
_____
_____
_____
_____
_____
_____
_____
_____
_____
_____
_____

Chapter 11
HOW DO YOU KNOW GOD?

The names of God reveal character traits of Jesus, the Christ. I once heard a minister teach that God had so many facets that when the angels fly around him, each time, they each see different character traits of God; and each time, in sheer and utter delight, they cry, "Holy, holy, holy is the most high God!"

Elohim means God of power and might, the only supreme and true God, and Creator (Genesis1:1).

Yahweh/Jehovah means the Lord, the proper name of the divine power, Intimate God (Hebrews 13:5, Exodus 3:14).

El Elyon means Most High God. God is above all gods; nothing in life is more sacred (Isaiah 14:13-14).

El Olam means the Everlasting God. God is eternal; he will never die (psalm 145:13).

El Roi means the God who sees and oversees all creation and the affairs of people. *El Roi* reveals the deep and secret things in its season.

El Shaddai means God Almighty, all sufficient and powerful. El Shaddai will change natural circumstances and creates miracles (Genesis 30:31-43).

Yahweh/Jehovah Rophe means the Lord, my healer, my deliverer. (Exodus 3:14). God heals our bodies (Acts 3:16), heals our situations (Exodus 15:23-25) and is even able to heal our nations (2 Chronicles 7:14).

Yahweh/Jehovah Jireh means the Lord will provide our real needs (Genesis 22:9-13).

Yahweh/Jehovah Rohi means the Lord is my Shepherd, and I shall not want. God provides our needs and wants. (Psalm 23:1-6).

Yahweh/Jehovah Nissi means the Lord, our Banner, helps us (Exodus 17:15).

Yahweh Elohim Yisrael means Lord God of Israel; he is the God of the nation (Genesis 12:2).

Yahweh/Jehovah Shalom means the Lord is Peace; he gives us peace, so we need not fear (Psalm 37:11).

Yahweh/Jehovah Makkeh means the Lord who Molds Me (Revelation 4:11).

Yahweh/Jehovah Sabaoth means Lord of Hosts (*Host* refers to armies but also to all the heavenly powers). God is our savior and protector (Isaiah 40:26).

Yahweh/Jehovah Tsidkenu means the Lord is our Righteousness. God is our standard for right behavior. He alone can make us righteous (Jeremiah 23:5-6).

Yahweh/Jehovah Shammah means the Lord is There. God is always present with us (Ezekiel 48:35).

Adonai means Lord. God alone is the head over all (Acts 2:36).

Attiq Yomin means Ancient of Days. God is the ultimate authority (Daniel 7:22).

Each of the names of God reveals different characteristics of God's nature that can meet your deepest needs and provide the warmest comfort.

Whom do you know God as? How has God manifested himself in your life? I want to fellowship with you in Heaven; if you are not saved, please confess the prayers below:

A Prayer of Salvation

"Father, it is written in your Word that Jesus came to seek and save the lost. His resurrection from the grave redeems us from all the curses of life and death. Father, you wish all men to be saved and to know your truth. Father, I ask that you move on the hearts of those who are interested in knowing you better to invite you into their hearts as their Savior and fi ll them with your Holy Spirit. Father, clothe them with the garment of salvation and the robe of righteousness. Jesus, please become Lord over my spirit, my soul, and my body. I do not fret or have anxiety about anything, and I take no cares of this world. Father, I pray that I learn and know your voice, hear your voice, and obey your voice. Amen."

The Need for Repentance

God desires truth in the inward parts and commands all men everywhere to repent (Psalm 51:6, Acts 17:30). The sinner must repent before he can become the recipient of salvation by grace through faith (Ephesians 2:8–9).

"He who covers his sins will not prosper, but whoever confesses and forsakes his sins will receive mercy" (Proverb 28:13).

Repentance is a gift from God; the goodness of God leads you to repentance. Repentance is an inward change produced by the convicting power of the Holy Spirit. The results are repentance toward God and faith toward our Lord Jesus Christ: faith that Christ died for our sins, that Christ was buried, and that he rose from the dead. Glory to God!

A Prayer to Repent from the Appearance of Prosperity and to be Made Whole

"My Father, *Abba*, I thank you that your life-giving Spirit hovers over me, dwells within me, and brings wisdom, favor, and understanding to me. I thank you that your lifegiving Spirit gives me direction and builds strength, instills knowledge, and reverence of you. I repent of living a worldly life obsessed, motivated, and driven by the appearance of the world's prosperity. God, I ask for your forgiveness, and I now establish my life upon the Word. Lord, send your angels before me to make the rough places smooth, make darkness light, and the crooked places straight. Lord, send your angels before me to make a river in the desert and a road in the wilderness. My God, you are my refuge and fortress. In you, only I trust. Make me whole. Father, I repent of all my sins and transgressions. I know the voice of the Lord. I hear the voice of the Lord, and I obey the voice of Lord. I am a believer and not a doubter. Please forgive me and make me whole, *Abba* Father." Amen. Selah.

Grace is underserved mercy and love. Our righteousness is because of Christ's righteousness. Is there anything in your life too hard for God? Is there anything too big for God? Is there anything too difficult for God? The answer to those questions is no. Our God is sufficient for all things, and he knows the end from the beginning of all things.

Jesus is the great I AM. He says to you, "I AM whatever you need me to be, whenever you need me."

Please, try Jesus. You have tried everything else! Peace.
Amen.

What has God revealed to you in chapter 11? Did you catch any new revelations?

Printed by Libri Plureos GmbH in Hamburg, Germany